Library Technology
REPORTS
Expert Guides to Library Systems and Services

Video Accessibility

Carli Spina

ALA TechSource
alatechsource.org

American Library Association

Library Technology REPORTS

ALA TechSource purchases fund advocacy, awareness, and accreditation programs for library professionals worldwide.

Volume 57, Number 3

Video Accessibility
ISBN: 978-0-8389-4823-1
DOI: https://doi.org/10.5860/ltr.57n3

American Library Association

225 N. Michigan Ave., Suite 1300
Chicago, IL 60601-7616 USA
alatechsource.org
800-545-2433, ext. 4299
312-944-6780
312-280-5275 (fax)

Advertising Representative

Patrick Hogan
phogan@ala.org
312-280-3240

Editor

Patrick Hogan
phogan@ala.org
312-280-3240

Copy Editor

Judith Lauber

Production

ALA Production Services

Cover Design

Alejandra Diaz and ALA Production Services

Library Technology Reports (ISSN 0024-2586) is published eight times a year (January, March, April, June, July, September, October, and December) by American Library Association, 225 N. Michigan Ave., Suite 1300, Chicago, IL 60601-7616. It is managed by ALA TechSource, a unit of the publishing department of ALA. Periodical postage paid at Chicago, Illinois, and at additional mailing offices. POSTMASTER: Send address changes to Library Technology Reports, 225 N. Michigan Ave., Suite 1300, Chicago, IL 60601-7616.

ALA TechSource
alatechsource.org

About the Author

Carli Spina is an associate professor and the head of Research & Instructional Services at SUNY's Fashion Institute of Technology (FIT) Library in New York City. She specializes in accessibility, universal design, user experience, and copyright. She is the author of the forthcoming book *Creating Inclusive Libraries by Applying Universal Design* and regularly teaches courses and workshops on accessibility and universal design.

Abstract

Video content is an increasingly important part of library marketing, outreach, instruction, and more. In order for this content to be inclusive for all patrons, it is vital that it be made accessible. However, large quantities of video content are still shared without adequate accessibility features, such as captions, transcriptions, audio descriptions, sign language interpretation, and accessible media players. This issue of *Library Technology Reports* (vol. 57, no. 3), "Video Accessibility," will help librarians to understand these various accessibility features and how they are used. It will also give them the knowledge and tools necessary to ensure that the videos they share, create, and purchase for their collections are accessible to all patrons.

Subscriptions

Contents

Contents, continued

Chapter 1

Why Is Video Accessibility Important?

Video content is an integral part of the modern online experience. Whether you are reading the news, searching for reviews of a product, or using a library database, chances are you will encounter video content. Even without considering the ever-increasing number of online services devoted to streaming video, the simple fact of the matter is that video is everywhere online. Streaming seasons of television shows, the latest Hollywood movies, product reviews, cute cat videos, and everything in between are found on the internet. In fact, research has shown that over 500 hours of video were uploaded to YouTube alone every minute in May 2019,[1] and this number has likely only increased as more activities moved online in the spring of 2020 during the COVID-19 pandemic.

It's easy to understand why video content is proliferating so quickly. It can be a dynamic way to reach a wide range of audiences. In some cases, it can also be the fastest way to convey complex information. Most of all, internet users are less likely to scan past an auto-playing video without absorbing some of the content than they are to skip over a line of text. In addition, the tools for creating video are continually growing less expensive and more user-friendly. That means that more people can share their message via video than ever before.

As a result, many content producers, from companies selling products to news organizations to individual creators, have put an increasing emphasis on video production and dissemination. The data suggests that this trend will continue. By 2018, 85 percent of internet users in the United States watched online video, including 50 percent who watched online videos daily, and by 2020, the total number of digital video viewers in the United States was 232 million.[2] The data suggests that this focus on video is only going to continue to increase. Cisco Systems, Inc., a major international telecommunications and network solutions corporation, predicts that by 2022, video will make up 82 percent of all internet traffic.[3] It's clear that video content will not disappear from the internet anytime soon.

But Who Can Use It?

With video making up such an important segment of internet usage, the question of whether this content is accessible gains urgency, particularly given how many people are impacted. Worldwide, 15 percent of the population has a disability.[4] In the United States, that number is even higher, at 26 percent of the total national population.[5] For some of these individuals, video may be more accessible than other methods of conveying information. For example, users with disabilities that impact reading may prefer watching a video to reading a text on the same subject.

However, for many users, video content presents significant accessibility barriers if it is not formatted properly and designed to include features such as captions, audio descriptions, and transcripts. People with different types of disabilities experience barriers to the use of videos when these elements are omitted, including those who are D/deaf or hard of hearing, those who have limited vision, and those with sound-processing or cognition disabilities. It is estimated that in the United States, 5.9 percent of the population is D/deaf or hard of hearing and 4.6 percent of the population is blind or has serious vision issues that aren't fully correctable with surgery or corrective lens, which gives some sense of the size of the overall population that relies on accessible video content.[6] Beyond these numbers, users who do not identify as disabled can also benefit from these features, including aging users who may have experienced changes to their vision or hearing and those for whom English is not their primary language.

Unfortunately, much online web content remains inaccessible. As a whole, web accessibility remains uneven. A recent study of one million home pages of top websites found that 98.1 percent of them had accessibility issues that could be detected through automated testing.[7] Video content is also frequently inaccessible. Some video platforms still do not offer integrated captioning functionality, which makes it difficult to add captions and impossible to offer closed captions. Even fewer platforms offer support for separate audio tracks featuring audio descriptions. This fact means that the only way to offer audio descriptions in many platforms is to integrate them in the main audio track used by all viewers. While there are often options for offering transcripts for videos, many of those that are offered online are formatted in ways that limit their accessibility, especially for those who use assistive devices. However, recently there has been a move toward greater awareness about these issues, which means that the tools for improving video accessibility are growing more robust all the time. Creators have an ever-expanding number of options for offering more inclusive access to their content.

Video in Libraries

Just as video content is important on the internet as a whole, it is a central element of many libraries' content, and accordingly, it is important that libraries consider questions related to video accessibility. Libraries offer video in many different ways, with varying levels of control over that content. This fact makes it vital that libraries understand how best to ensure that their video content is usable and accessible by all of their patrons and does not unintentionally exclude some from the information shared in this medium.

Much of the video content offered to patrons by libraries is delivered via vendor products to which the library subscribes. For this content, the library may not have the power to make the video accessible within the database, but it should still consider accessibility as a factor in selecting products and have a plan in place for improving access. In addition, libraries have a strong role in advocating with vendors for better quality content and negotiating contracts that require that videos meet their standards.

Libraries have the most control over video content when the content is owned, created, or hosted by the library. Such content can encompass everything from social media posts to video tutorials for archival content. Though the precise features needed to ensure that this content is accessible may vary based on the specifics of each video, libraries that are stewarding this type of video content must have workflows in place to address its accessibility. This issue of *Library Technology Reports* will explain the elements of video accessibility and offer advice for those interested in addressing these topics at their libraries.

Notes

1. J. Clement, "Hours of Video Uploaded to YouTube Every Minute 2007–2019," Statista, August 25, 2020, https://www.statista.com/statistics/259477/hours-of-video-uploaded-to-youtube-every-minute# (requires subscription).
2. J. Clement, "Online Video Usage in the United States—Statistics & Facts," Statista, September 30, 2019, https://www.statista.com/topics/1137/online-video (requires subscription).
3. Thomas Barnett, Jr., Shruti Jain, Usha Andra, and Taru Khurana, "Cisco Visual Networking Index (VNI) Complete Forecast Update, 2017–2022," APJC Cisco Knowledge Network (CKN) presentation, December 2018, https://www.cisco.com/c/dam/m/en_us/network-intelligence/service-provider/digital-transformation/knowledge-network-webinars/pdfs/1213-business-services-ckn.pdf.
4. The World Bank, "Disability Inclusion," May 15, 2020, https://www.worldbank.org/en/topic/disability.
5. Centers for Disease Control and Prevention, (2019, September 9). "Disability Impacts All of Us" (infographic), September 9, 2019, https://www.cdc.gov/ncbddd/disabilityandhealth/infographic-disability-impacts-all.html.
6. Centers for Disease Control and Prevention, "Disability Impacts All of Us."
7. "The WebAIM Million," WebAIM, last updated March 30, 2020, https://webaim.org/projects/million.

Chapter 2

Captions

Most people have encountered video captioning at some point. Whether on a TV show at a noisy restaurant or on a YouTube video, captions are often around without most viewers giving them much thought. Those who have stopped to consider captions may think of them as an accessibility feature but may not have considered what goes into optimizing their usability. For video creators, however, it is important to understand what captions are, why they are important, and what makes them effective.

What Are Captions?

In the video context, captions can be defined as "one or two lines of text, which represent approximately 1–2 seconds of audio, . . . overlaid on the video screen, which can sometimes obscure video visuals."[1] The captions stay on the screen long enough to be read while moving quickly enough to maintain synchronization with the content of the audio track. It is important to note that this definition refers not simply to spoken content but to all audio content. An important part of captions is translating necessary sound effects and similar audio content, in addition to the spoken language, into text.

As a result, captioning can be a more subjective process than most may realize. This is particularly true in the case of content with noteworthy background sounds where the captioner must decide which background content should be described in the captions and how it should be described. As Sean Zdenek explains it, "Captioning is about meaning, not sound per se. Captions don't describe sounds so much as convey the purpose and meaning of sounds in specific contexts."[2] While for many types of video content, transcribing the contents of the dialogue may be sufficient to capture the full meaning of the audio track, it is important not to fall into the assumption that transcribing dialogue by itself is necessarily sufficient (figure 2.1). To be effective, captions must recreate the experience of listening to the audio content for those who cannot or do not wish to do so. If the captions do not fully represent that content, they will not offer an equivalent experience that is inclusive for those who need or prefer to use captions when viewing video content.

Captions and Subtitles: What's the Difference?

In the United States, the term *captions* typically refers to text that represents the audio in the same language as that audio content, while *subtitles*, on the other hand, refers to text that translates the dialogue into another language. Unlike captions, subtitles typically do not include a textual representation of sound effects and other nonspoken audio content because there is an assumption that the primary users for subtitles will be hearing users who do not fully understand the language but are otherwise able to perceive the audio elements of the video.

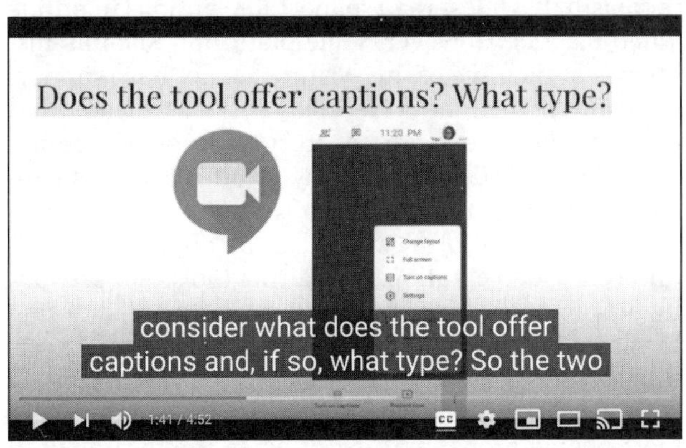

Figure 2.1
Example of closed captions

This distinction is not standard around the world. In many languages and countries, including in many cases in the United Kingdom, the term *subtitles* is used to refer to both types of textual representation of audio content. In these cases, the distinction between the terms is sometimes indicated by referring to text that translates the audio from one language to another as *interlingual subtitles*, while referring to content in the same language as *intralingual subtitles*. In some formal circumstances, this terminology can also be used in the United States, though it is significantly less common. While interlingual subtitles can fulfill some of the purposes of intralingual subtitles or captions, they are not frequently created with accessibility in mind and therefore likely will not fulfill the primary purpose of captions.

Open Captions versus Closed Captions

Captions can be displayed in one of two manners: (1) *Open Captions*, which are permanently visible on the video and cannot be removed, or (2) *Closed Captions*, which can be toggled on or off at the option of the user. Open captions are sometimes also known as *hard-coded captions*, *baked-in captions*, or *burnt-in captions* because they are integrally a part of the video content. One common use of open captions is in live performances, such as theatrical performances, where the audio content is captioned on a screen often above the stage. One advantage of open captions is that the video will always be accessible to those who are D/deaf or hard of hearing without the need for the person controlling the video player to turn on captions. This can be particularly useful in environments such as classrooms or conferences, where the person playing the video may not be aware of the needs of all audience members. In an online environment, open captions also do not require that the video player be compatible with captions. At this point, there is increasingly widespread support for captions in online video players. However, some platforms, such as Instagram at the time of this writing, do not have support for captions in their video players. This means that captions that users can opt to turn on or off are not possible. Instead, the only way to offer captions is to embed open captions in video content before uploading it to the platform, which can be done with many different video creation and editing tools. A disadvantage of open captions is that they can be distracting for users with certain types of disabilities and in certain settings.

Closed captions are the version of captions that most people probably think of when the term is used because they are prevalent both online and off. They are often denoted by one of two symbols, either two *C*s next to each other (figure 2.2), sometimes surrounded by the outline of a screen or television, or the "slashed ear" symbol, which is an icon of an ear with a line through it. This second symbol is also used to indicate services for those who are D/deaf or hard of hearing more generally, but in some parts of the world, or some contexts, it can specifically indicate closed captions. The primary advantage of closed captions is that they allow the viewer to decide whether or not captions are displayed for each individual video based on their specific needs. Many video players also allow users to set persistent preferences if they regularly use captions. The disadvantage of closed captions is that users may not realize they are available, may not know how to turn them on, or, in the case of group viewing of a video, may not realize that some viewers require or prefer captions. Though less of a problem with modern online videos and on televisions in the United States, another potential disadvantage of closed captions is that they require a compatible player to display the captions.

Figure 2.2
Closed caption symbol

A Brief History of Video Captioning

When films initially emerged, they were silent and were inherently accessible to those who could not hear. However, with the emergence of sound films, an access problem arose that was not meaningfully addressed for some time. In 1958, a law was passed to establish a Captioned Films for the Deaf program that loaned captioned films to groups of D/deaf and hard of hearing viewers.[3] Eventually, captions moved to the small screen. The first instance of open captioned content on television was rebroadcast episodes of Julia Child's *The French Chef*, which started on WGBH in 1972, followed by the debut of open captioned rebroadcasts of *ABC World News Tonight* on the same channel.[4] It was not until 1980 that closed captions debuted on American television, and by the late 1990s over 500 hours of captioned programming was broadcast each week.[5] Though it may be surprising that open captions preceded closed captions by so many years, this is because it was not until the Television Decoder Circuitry Act of 1990 that all televisions with a thirteen-inch or larger screen in the US were required to have the technology necessary to support closed captions.[6] Prior to that, those who wanted to access closed captions needed external equipment, which limited the reach of the technology, particularly in public spaces where captions are often seen today, such as airports and restaurants.

With the advent of online streaming video, captions became important for a new type of video that offered access to new types of content. One of many ways in which online video is different from television programs is that more of it is created by individuals or institutions that may not have much experience or expertise in video creation, which likely contributed to the lag in captioned video online. However, there were other significant factors, including a lack of support for closed captions on online video platforms such as YouTube, which did not have support for closed captions until 2008.[7] In recent years, lawsuits have helped to expand the availability of captions, including influential lawsuits filed by the National Association of the Deaf against Netflix, Harvard, and MIT, which helped advance online captioning significantly.[8] Though the availability of captioned online videos has increased, there are still many uncaptioned, inaccessible videos available online and even entire platforms that either do not support captions or offer only minimal access for users.

Why Is Captioning Important?

From an accessibility point of view, captioning is vital for users who are D/deaf or hard of hearing, and these users should always be the top priority when designing captions and media player support for captions. Given that about 15 percent of the population of the United States has at least some difficulty hearing, this constitutes a significant audience. Including captions makes video content more inclusive for these users. It also fulfills basic legal requirements that many organizations must meet, especially government and educational institutions.

However, D/deaf and hard-of-hearing users are hardly the only audience for captions. Many different users find captions useful in many different settings, including

- users who process information better through text;
- users who need or want to watch videos without the audio on, whether due to their setting, such as when watching in a library, or to not disturb others around them;
- users for whom the language of the video is not their primary language, particularly when subtitles are not available;
- users watching videos with speakers who mumble, with unclear audio tracks, or with speakers with multiple accents;
- users learning new terms or concepts that might be easier to comprehend either through text or a mix of text and audio; and
- users who are learning to read.

Data shows that captions are popular in these and other situations. A 2019 study of consumers 18 to 54 years of age by Verizon Media and Publicis Media found that 80 percent of those using captions are not D/deaf or hard of hearing but are actually using captions for another reason.[9] The same study also found that 80 percent of respondents said that the presence of captions made them more likely to watch a video.[10] Other studies have also found that captions impact viewership. A study by 3Play Media and Discovery Digital Networks (DDN) found that there was an "overall increase of 7.32% in views for captioned videos" on DDN's YouTube channel.[11] A nationwide study of students at institutions of higher education found that 70.8 percent of surveyed students who did not have any type of hearing difficulty used closed captions when watching at least some of the videos associated with their courses.[12] No matter the setting, it is clear that many users prefer to use captions.

Beyond their popularity, captions also offer benefits for virtually all users. In fact, a 2015 review of the literature found that over 100 empirical studies had shown benefits of captions for users of many ages and in many scenarios.[13] In educational settings, captions have been shown to be particularly useful. A study of caption use in language learning classes found that captions "result in greater depth of processing by focusing attention, reinforce the acquisition of vocabulary through multiple modalities, and allow learners to determine meaning through the unpacking of language chunks."[14] Beyond language learning, captions have been demonstrated to have notable benefits for students at many different levels, from elementary school to college.[15] While it is vital that users with disabilities remain the primary focus when designing video captions, it is equally clear that captions will be beneficial for many other users.

How Are Captions Created?

There are three primary ways that captions are created. Until recently, captions were almost always created by an individual typing up captions for the content during or after creation of the film or video. These individuals are sometimes referred to as stenocaptioners if they use stenography equipment for the process. This method can be used for both prerecorded content and live content. However, another way that captions can be created in some platforms is by typing up or uploading an existing script of the dialogue, either with time stamps built in or using a tool that is capable of detecting sounds and automatically lining up the captions. Using more recent technologies, captions can also be created using artificial intelligence (AI) word recognition. Well-known applications such as PowerPoint, Google Docs, Zoom, and YouTube have automatic captioning features built in to their programs. Though the idea of automatically generated captions is appealing, the accuracy of these automated tools still lags behind the accuracy that can be achieved by human-created captions, particularly when the audio is unclear for any number of reasons, from recording standards to the level of enunciation of speakers. Recent research demonstrates that this issue persists in particular in videos with technical terminology.[16] For many institutions, this automated approach to captioning must be combined with a human review after the fact to find and fix any errors. However, automatically generated captions are increasingly integrated into video conferencing tools to support captioning live events. Skilled stenocaptioners can provide more accurate real-time captions in many cases, and many of these platforms also provide an option for integrating captions created in this manner.

Caption Accuracy

Though it may seem obvious that captions should be an accurate representation of the audio content, views on the best approach to accuracy have changed over time. Initially when captions were aired on television, they intentionally did not exactly represent what was said in the video and instead edited the content to ensure that the captions were written at a lower reading level, a fact that some researchers have argued was accepted at that time at least in part because "deaf people were so delighted to have captions that they accepted almost anything thrown on the screen."[17] Over time, this model shifted significantly so that it is now much more common for captions to be defined as the "verbatim translation of spoken dialogue."[18] In fact, best practices are generally to offer 99 percent accuracy, a level that is offered by many vendors that provide commercial transcription and captioning services. This high level of accuracy is needed to ensure that the video is comprehensible for users who have no access to the audio track. For this reason, workflows that involve automated captions generally also need to incorporate a review to ensure the accuracy of the generated captions.

Though accuracy is vital, the meaning of accuracy can be more complicated than it might seem at first. One often-overlooked fact about captions is that they are, to at least some degree, subjective. While they should strive to recreate the sound of the video content, the final product may well differ, most particularly when there are non-dialogue elements integrated into the audio. In fact, there will often be more than one official set of professionally produced captions for a single movie or TV show that is released in different settings, such as a television broadcast and a DVD release. This is because captions are intended to translate the full spectrum of the sounds that are part of the video. They are meant to convey not only the meaning of dialogue that is unclear, and therefore subject to interpretation by the captioner, but also the important background sounds and sound effects, and in some cases a descriptor of a character's emotion. Any sound that conveys meaning is integrated into the captions for a video. As Zdenek argues, in at least some contexts, "captioners not only select which sounds are significant, and hence which sounds are worthy of being captioned, but also rhetorically invent words for sounds."[19] It is also important to note that, though the modern best practice is generally to caption all spoken words, captioners in some cases may be required to also rephrase or condense spoken content to reasonably be read by viewers during the duration of the relevant video content. All of these factors mean that some experts recommend employing experts to create captions for videos used in educational settings, though of course this has associated costs.

Best Practices for Caption Creation

For those who are interested in creating captions, there are some best practices that can help to ensure that the completed captions offer meaningful access for users:

- Accuracy is vital. Strive for 99 percent accuracy for prerecorded captions. When providing captions for a live event, strive for maximum accuracy and, if a recording will later be provided, correct the captions before providing access to the recorded video. When using automatic captioning features, check and correct captions as necessary to achieve 99 percent accuracy.
- Avoid obscuring important content in the video with the captions.
- Ensure that the font size of the captions is large enough to be comfortably read even by those with low vision. Generally, the font size recommended for accessibility is no smaller than 16 points, and captions should be one or two font sizes larger than that. However, that will vary depending on the size of the video, and not all platforms will allow the caption creator to select the size of the font.
- Choose a font that is very readable. Generally, sans serif fonts such as Arial, Helvetica, or Verdana are preferred for this purpose, though not all platforms offer multiple font options.
- Select a font color that will be high contrast compared to the video content if the captions will be overlaid over the video or high contrast compared to the background if the captions will be on a solid

background immediately below the video content. If the platform being used offers only a single caption color, it is important to consider where the captions will appear on the screen and attempt to ensure that the background behind the captions will offer a high contrast backdrop for the text.

- If at all possible, allow users the flexibility to select between several fonts, font sizes, and font colors to find the settings that work best for them. This feature is not supported by all video players, but it should be offered when supported.
- Censor only content that is censored in the audio track. For example, if profanity is bleeped out in the audio track, it should be similarly censored in the captions, but if it is not bleeped out in the audio track, it should not be censored. Content that is censored according to this model should be reflected either by replacing some letters in the middle of the word or by simply typing *[expletive]* in place of the word.
- Limit the number of words and characters on the screen at any time to ensure that the text is readable.
- Caption synchronization is important. The text on the screen should be closely synchronized with the audio track. In the case of prerecorded video content, this synchronization should be exact. When creating captions during a live event, complete synchronization is not possible, but synchronization should be as close as possible.
- The text should remain on the screen long enough to be readable. In the case of fast-moving dialogue, this may at times require some abridging and editing of the content. However, this should be done only when absolutely necessary as verbatim captions are preferable.
- Sounds indicating pauses or serving as fillers, such as *um*, *ah*, *hmm*, or similar, can be omitted as long as their omission does not prevent those reading the captions from understanding the meaning of the content. Similarly, if a speaker misspeaks or repeats a word, this may also be omitted if it does not impact the meaning of the content.
- Sound effects should be captioned in addition to dialogue. Similarly, captions should indicate when music is playing and should caption lyrics, particularly if they are relevant to the meaning of the content.
- In the case of dialogue where it is important to know who is speaking and this may be unclear to those viewing the video without sound, the captions should indicate this information. For example, if dialogue is spoken by someone off screen, this should be indicated.

Captions are a vital element of accessibility. While they are increasingly found in videos both online and offline, unfortunately, many videos still lack captions. The advent of automated captions on platforms such as YouTube has increased their prevalence, but issues of accuracy remain. In order to provide an equitable and usable viewing experience regardless of access to the audio track, it is important to incorporate accurate captions into all video content.

Notes

1. Raja S. Kushalnagar, Walter S. Lasecki, and Jeffrey P. Bigham, "Captions versus Transcripts for Online Video Content," in *W4A '13: Proceedings of the 10th International Cross-Disciplinary Conference on Web Accessibility*, 1, http://www.cs.cmu.edu/~jbigham/pubs/pdfs/2014/captionvstranscripts.pdf.
2. Sean Zdenek, *Reading Sounds: Closed-Captioned Media and Popular Culture* (Chicago: University of Chicago Press, 2015), 8.
3. Captioned Films Act of 1958, Pub. L. No. 85-905, 72 Stat. 1742 (1958).
4. Carl Jensema, Ralph McCann, and Scott Ramsey, "Closed-Captioned Television Presentation Speed and Vocabulary," *American Annals of the Deaf* 141, no. 4 (October 1996): 284.
5. Carl Jensema, "Viewer Reaction to Different Television Captioning Speeds," *American Annals of the Deaf* 143, no. 4 (October 1998): 318.
6. Television Decoder Circuitry Act of 1990, 47 U.S.C. §§ 303(u) and 330(b) (1990).
7. YouTube, "YouTube Captions and Subtitles," posted September 22, 2008, YouTube video, 1:36, https://www.youtube.com/watch?v=QRS8MkLhQmM.
8. National Association of the Deaf, "NAD Files Disability Civil Rights Lawsuit against Netflix," June 16, 2011, https://www.nad.org/2011/06/16/nad-files-disability-civil-rights-lawsuit-against-netflix; National Association of the Deaf, "Landmark Agreements Establish New Model for Online Accessibility in Higher Education and Business" (news release), February 18, 2020, https://www.nad.org/2020/02/18/landmark-agreements-establish-new-model-for-online-accessibility-in-higher-education-and-business.
9. Verizon Media, "Make Noise with the Right Digital Video Captioning" (infographic), April 2019, https://b2b.verizonmedia.com/c/verizon-media-sound--1?x=vOJKbY.
10. Verizon Media, "Make Noise."
11. 3Play Media, "Discovery Digital Networks," accessed October 24, 2020, https://www.3playmedia.com/why-3play/case-studies/discovery-digital-networks.
12. Katie Linder, *Student Uses and Perceptions of Closed Captions and Transcripts: Results from a National Study* (Corvallis: Oregon State University Ecampus Research Unit, October 2016).
13. Morton Ann Gernsbacher, "Video Captions Benefit Everyone," *Policy Insights from the Behavioral and Brain Sciences* 2, no. 1 (2015): 195–202.
14. Paula Winke, Susan Gass, and Tetyana Syodorenko, "The Effects of Captioning Videos Used for Foreign Language Listening Activities," *Language Learning and Technology* 14, no. 1 (2010): 81.
15. Faye Parkhill, Jiliane Johnson, and Jane Bates,

"Capturing Literacy Learners: Evaluating a Reading Programme Using Popular Novels and Films with Subtitles," *Digital Culture and Education* 3, no. 2 (2011): 140–56; Aaron Steinfeld, "The Benefit of Real-Time Captioning in a Mainstream Classroom as Measured by Working Memory," *Volta Review* 100, no. 1 (1998): 29–44.

16. Tharindu R. Liyanagunawardena, "Automatic Transcription Software: Good Enough for Accessibility? A Case Study from Built Environment Education," in *European Distance and E-Learning Network (EDEN) Proceedings: EDEN 2019 Annual Conference, Bruges, Belgium*, ed. Airina Volungeviciene and András Szűcs (Budapest, Hungary: European Distance and E-Learning Network, 2019), 388–96.
17. Jensema, McCann, and Ramsey, "Closed-Captioned Presentation Speed and Vocabulary," 285.
18. John-Patrick Udo and Deborah I. Fels, "The Rogue Poster-Children of Universal Design: Closed Captioning and Audio Description," *Journal of Engineering Design* 21, no. 2–3 (2010): 207.
19. Zdenek, *Reading Sounds*, 1.

Chapter 3

Transcripts

Transcripts are an important element of the video accessibility landscape, even though they are not as commonly considered as captions. Often mistakenly seen as nothing more than an alternative to captions, transcripts can serve separate and equally important purposes for both accessibility and usability. In many cases, it makes sense to offer them as another access point rather than seeing them as merely an alternative to existing accessibility options. Transcripts serve as an excellent example of the way that providing multiple accessibility features also offers better, more versatile, and more flexible user experiences for everyone.

What Are Transcripts?

As with captions, transcripts represent in textual form the audible content included in videos and other multimedia content. In order to serve as a complete replacement for this audio content, transcripts generally include textual descriptions or representations of important sounds beyond speech. The primary distinction between transcripts and captions is how and where they are displayed.

> Transcripts show many lines of text representing several seconds of audio, but cannot be overlaid on the video screen, as the text would obscure too much information. So they are shown in a separate window, next to or under the video screen, but this can also be hard to read as the text is further away from the video.[1]

Because transcripts are not directly connected to the video and can be used without viewing the video, they often include textual representations of important visual content from the video as well. This type of transcript is sometimes referred to as a *descriptive transcript.*

Transcripts can be presented completely separately from the video content, but in online environments, it is more common for them to appear to the side of or below the video player in a location that allows users to read them while viewing the video (figure 3.1). While transcripts can simply be a static presentation of text, an increasing number of online transcripts scroll in sync with the video content or allow users to navigate through video content by clicking on specific sections of the transcript, which adds greater interactivity for users. Transcripts that facilitate moving through the video can be particularly useful for long videos as they allow users to refer back to specific sections without viewing the entire video again.

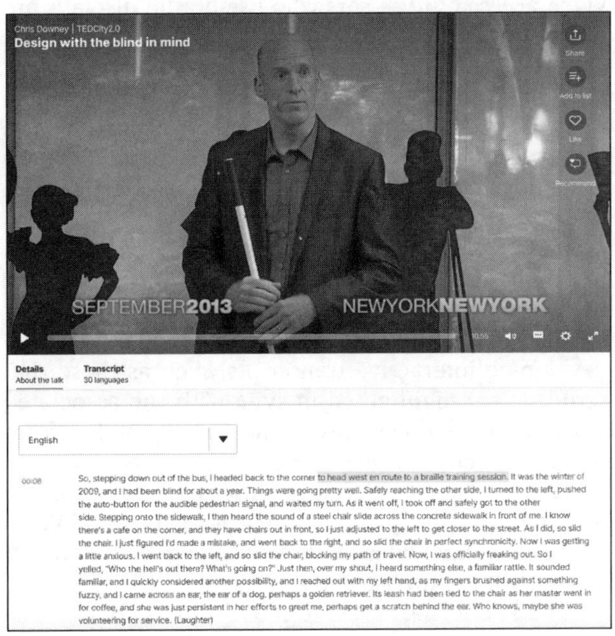

Figure 3.1
Example of an interactive transcript

The Role of Transcripts in Accessibility

Among video accessibility options, transcripts are frequently overlooked. Many see them as an inferior substitute for captions. It is true that transcripts are less effective for users who hope to read a textual narrative while simultaneously watching the video content. As noted above, the text is displayed separately from the video, which can be a less usable setup for most users. Though there are display options that can help to mitigate this issue, such as a display that features transcripts that scroll in sync with the video just to the side of the video content, it does mean that transcripts are rarely an optimal replacement for captions. Even when they are positioned carefully and scroll with the video, they are still generally not the preferred choice for many of the main audiences for captions, including D/deaf or hard-of-hearing users and those watching the video with the sound turned off.

However, this understanding of the utility of transcripts misses the important roles that transcripts play in video usability and accessibility. Of particular importance is the fact that transcripts are vital for deafblind or blind individuals who use braille displays. Because video captions are integrated into the video themselves, they cannot be read by braille displays in most, if not all, situations. This leaves these videos inaccessible to users who access content with this type of assistive technology. In particular, for users who are deafblind, transcripts may be their only option for accessing videos. This specific need is one that is still overlooked at a greater rate than other types of online video accessibility. Users who use braille displays are best served by offering transcripts in addition to, or even instead of, captions. To make the video content accessible to these users, transcripts must include information about the visual elements of the video as well, meaning that descriptive transcripts offer a significantly better and more equitable user experience for these users.

In addition, for deafblind users, it is not enough to simply offer transcripts, but those transcripts must be placed and carefully designed for maximum accessibility. Especially for those who are interested in developing interactive transcripts, such as those that scroll or are highlighted in sync with the associated video, accessible web design must be at the forefront if the transcripts are intended to provide access for users who use assistive tools. Too often captions are presented in a way that makes them inaccessible to assistive technologies, such as braille displays, which severely limits their utility.

While offering access to those who use braille displays is perhaps the most noteworthy function for transcripts, because braille displays may be the sole access point for those users, there are other accessibility advantages to offering transcripts in addition to captions. Users with certain types of learning disabilities may find that they prefer, and learn better from, reading the content as compared to watching a video. In particular, transcripts can be useful for those who may have difficulty processing auditory information or those who may find captions distracting or confusing while watching a video. Offering transcripts ensures that the needs of all of these users are addressed so that ultimately the informative content in the video is accessible and usable by a wider segment of the intended audience.

The Role of Transcripts in Usability

Some users may find that they simply prefer reading a transcript because they can read or scan it more quickly than they can watch a video. This is particularly helpful for users who are approaching video content for education or research purposes, as transcripts are fully searchable, allow for faster skimming when reviewing the information, and can most easily be added into notes by cutting and pasting direct quotations. In many cases, these use cases are independent reasons that transcripts are useful in educational settings. Even aside from their value for accessibility, transcripts are worthwhile because of the many ways that they can provide an improved user experience when they are offered in addition to captions on video content.

Transcripts can also be preferable for those with low bandwidth or unstable internet connections who struggle to load and watch video content online. They also work better for those users who simply don't want to or cannot afford to pay for the data usage necessary to download a video, particularly in a mobile environment. None of these groups are well served by captions as they require that the user download or stream the video to access its content, which may not be technologically possible for them.

In addition, "creation of transcription for audio information allows audio data to be manipulated, archived, and retrieved more efficiently because text-based search is more expedient than audio-based search,"[2] and caption files are often not available to these sorts of activities and the tools that facilitate them. As a result, transcripts are more versatile for other uses of the content, including analyzing text, running searches, and integrating content into other projects. Facilitating these uses can help to foster creative reuses of the video content and can ensure that it is available for unanticipated future needs. In addition, transcripts improve the search engine optimization for video content, making it more findable by potential users.

While this issue of *Library Technology Reports* is focused on the features and technologies needed to make video content accessible, it is worthwhile to note here that transcripts serve an important role in the accessibility of audio-only content as well. With the increasing popularity of online audio content generally, and podcasts specifically, transcripts are increasingly relevant for this purpose. It is important to note, though, that as with video content, unfortunately much of the audio content that is published frequently is not made accessible at the time of publication, with accessibility features added later as an afterthought. Transcripts for audio-only content make it accessible to users who are D/deaf or hard of hearing as well as improving search engine optimization, allowing users to search through the content. They also offer an option for those who prefer to read their information, just as in the case of videos. In fact, one study found that when *This American Life* added transcripts to its content, "the number of unique visitors who discovered TAL through organic search results increased by 6.68%."[3]

Best Practices for Transcript Creation

Because the nature of transcripts means that they may be used separately from, or instead of, the video content rather than in tandem with it, transcripts must do more than simply reproduce the audio content of the video to be effective. In some ways, transcript creators should aim to accurately reflect both the audio elements and the key visual elements of the video. This is somewhat akin to combining the content of both captions and audio descriptions (discussed further in chapter 4). Some important best practices for creating high-quality transcripts are as follows:

- Ensure that all of the audio content is captured exactly as presented. All speech should be reproduced exactly as spoken. Unlike captions, there is less concern with transcripts if the content is lengthy because there is no need for it to fit on the screen in time with the audio. For this reason, transcripts should be as faithful as possible to the spoken content and should not be edited, abridged, or abbreviated unless absolutely necessary.
- The only time that audio content should be omitted is when it is inaudible. In these cases, there should be an indication that there is an inaudible sound. Such an indication could be used for characters who are whispering inaudibly or mumbling to themselves, for example.
- Spoken content should be presented as in the video, meaning that content should be censored only if it is also censored in the audio track of the video file.
- Indicate who the speaker is, when the speaker changes, and if the speaker is off screen to give context for those who are not viewing the video.
- Tone, emphasis, and other noteworthy features, such as volume, should be conveyed as appropriate, using punctuation or other consistently used characters. These features should be indicated with text only when it is impossible to otherwise indicate them.
- Indicate important sounds other than speech and their source.
- Specifically for music, indicate relevant information about the track, such as title and artist or even the full lyrics if this information is relevant in the context of the video.
- Indicate important visual information in the transcript by integrating it into the text. For example, describe what is happening on screen or the information silently presented on screen. This process should be similar to the process of deciding what information should be included in audio descriptions.

It is important to view transcripts as more than an alternative to captions. Though that is one role that they can play, there are many others as well. Rather than serving as a replacement for other accessibility features, they have their own benefits and expand the number of people for whom the content is usable. They can also make the content available for more types of uses both now and in the future.

As with so many aspects of accessibility, the importance of transcripts can be an example of the value in offering multiple options. Each user is different, whether or not they have a disability or use assistive technologies. They all have personal preferences and individualized technology setups, which may or may not involve assistive technologies. Because of these variations among users, offering flexibility and multiple access methods for the video content and the information it conveys is the best way to make this content widely accessible and usable. While this advice generally applies to the design and configuration of any presentation, it is particularly relevant in the case of video content, where the medium itself presents unique challenges for certain users. Wherever possible, the best approach is to integrate transcripts in addition to other access solutions to offer users options that will work best for their specific needs.

Notes

1. Raja S. Kushalnagar, Walter S. Lasecki, and Jeffrey P. Bigham. "Captions versus Transcripts for Online Video Content," in *W4A '13: Proceedings of the 10th International Cross-Disciplinary Conference on Web Accessibility* (New York: Association for Computing Machinery, 2013), 1, http://www.cs.cmu.edu/~jbigham/pubs/pdfs/2014/captionvstranscripts.pdf.

2. Keith Bain, Sara Basson, Alexander Faisman, and Dimitri Kanevsky, "Accessibility, Transcription, and Access Everywhere," *IBM Systems Journal* 44, no. 3 (2005): 598.
3. 3Play Media, "This American Life," accessed October 24, 2020, https://www.3playmedia.com/why-3play/case-studies/this-american-life.

Chapter 4

Audio Descriptions

While most people have encountered captioned videos, audio descriptions remain less well known. Unfortunately, they are also less prevalent than captions across virtually all platforms. It is important that video creators strive to address this disparity by including audio descriptions in their content where needed, but the first step in this process is understanding what audio descriptions are, how they differ from captions, and what is required to provide high-quality audio descriptions.

What Are Audio Descriptions?

Audio description can go by several different names, which all refer to the same concept, including *video description*, *described video*, *audio described video*, *verbal description*, *visual description*, *audio-narrated description*, and *descriptive narration*. However, *audio description* is used most frequently, particularly in the United States, where this has been the preferred term of several government institutions.

Regardless of the terminology used, the basic concept remains the same. Audio description is defined by the US Access Board as

> Narration added to the soundtrack to describe important visual details that cannot be understood from the main soundtrack alone. Audio description is a means to inform individuals who are blind or who have low vision about visual content essential for comprehension. Audio description of video provides information about actions, characters, scene changes, on-screen text, and other visual content. Audio description supplements the regular audio track of a program. Audio description is usually added during existing pauses in dialogue.[1]

A similar definition appears in the documentation for the Web Content Accessibility Guidelines (WCAG) 2.1, which also notes that audio description is not necessary where all the visual information is already explained in the audio track,[2] for example, a video that shows text on the screen that is read as part, or all, of the main audio track. Considering this example can help to clarify the purpose and importance of audio description. It is a means of representing the visual information of a video in an alternate format that allows it to be perceived by another sense. The symbol for audio description is shown in figure 4.1.

While audio description is primarily used to make video content accessible, it can also be used in other settings to improve accessibility. In any arena where visual elements are key, audio description can be adapted as a method of access. It has been used to improve the accessibility of museums, art displays, fashion shows, parades, dance performances, fireworks displays, video games, and virtual reality experiences. Overall, it is a very versatile process that can be adapted to many different settings even though it is primarily thought of as a tool for improving video accessibility.

Figure 4.1
Audio description symbol

Why Is Audio Description Important?

For most video content, the visual information presented on the screen is not represented in the audio track. This information remains unknown to anyone who is unable to see the video. Audio descriptions are, therefore, vital to make this content accessible to those whose vision makes it impossible for them to perceive the visual information of the video.

While many people might think that the audience for audio descriptions consists solely of those who are completely unable to see, this stereotypical assumption about what it means to be blind or visually impaired is overly restrictive. For this reason, the National Federation of the Blind "encourage[s] people to consider themselves as blind if their sight is bad enough—even with corrective lenses—that they must use alternative methods to engage in any activity that people with normal vision would do using their eyes."[3] In the United States, there are approximately half a million children under the age of eighteen and almost twenty-seven million adults over the age of eighteen who are blind or visually impaired. Worldwide, over 250 million people have vision impairments. For these people, audio descriptions are vital to allow them to participate in visual content, whether a Hollywood blockbuster or educational videos assigned in their classes. Without audio descriptions, they must rely on merely the sound content of the video, which in many cases may be incomprehensible without the visual elements, or rely on finding someone who can describe the video to them. Audio descriptions offer meaningful, independent opportunities to interact with video for a segment of the population that is otherwise excluded.

Audio descriptions can also be useful to improve the experience of users who are able to view the content being described. As Joel Snyder has argued, audio description "is useful for anyone who wants to truly notice and appreciate a more full perspective on any visual event."[4] It can be useful particularly as an educational tool, as it draws attention to the most central and important visual elements of the content in a way that can help teach viewers how to recognize, describe, and understand these elements. However, just as audio description is not yet as common as captioning, its use by those who can see the content is not as common as the use of captions by those who can hear the audio.

In some countries, audio descriptions may be legally required in specific circumstances. For example, in the United States, the Federal Communications Commission has set standards pursuant to the 21st Century Communications and Video Accessibility Act that require TV stations to provide access to minimum amounts of audio described content.[5] In addition, the Justice Department has issued rules saying that specific types of movie theaters must support audio description to be in compliance with the Americans with Disabilities Act (ADA).[6] While neither of these rules specifically states whether audio descriptions are required for online video content, the fact that the ADA requires equitable access to public accommodations has led some to argue that audio descriptions are required for institutions that are subject to these legal provisions, particularly government entities.[7]

From a standards point of view, audio descriptions are also important. WCAG provides the framework for web accessibility standards for many institutions, and audio descriptions are incorporated into these guidelines. In order to achieve Level A compliance, WCAG 2.1 requires audio description or a "media alternative" for prerecorded media in most situations.[8] To achieve Level AA compliance, all prerecorded video must have audio description.[9] Interestingly, Level AAA compliance requires extended audio descriptions, which refers to audio descriptions that take longer than the natural pauses in the course of the main audio track.[10] These may not be needed in all video content, but they can be useful in cases where additional details would provide better access to the content.

A Brief History of Audio Descriptions

The concept of verbally describing the content of films is not a new one. An early example was the verbal description of a 1929 showing of a film for members of the New York Association for the Blind and the New York League for the Hard of Hearing.[11] After the event, the idea percolated from a few different independent sources. Chet Avery of the Department of Education was among the first to suggest the idea in the 1960s, and it was then independently the subject of a master's thesis that proposed that audio descriptions should be offered over the radio in sync with programs on television.[12] In the 1980s, audio description work began to gather interest in the world of theater,[13] which later led to interest in incorporating these descriptions into television programming. In the mid-1980s, Margaret Pfanstiehl, who had worked on description for theater programming, partnered with Barry Cronin, who had independently had the idea for audio description of television.[14] WGBH, Boston's PBS channel, "creat[ed] a national video description service by training describers" in efforts that would ultimately lead to WGBH funding its Descriptive Video Service in 1988.[15] This work was also done by two other organizations founded in the same year, which worked on television, video, and, notably, educational videos.[16]

In the online environment, audio descriptions have also become somewhat more prevalent than in the past. When streaming videos debuted, few had audio descriptions associated with them. However, access to them has begun to improve with major streaming video players incorporating audio descriptions in some of their content. Tools and services also exist to support the creation and sharing of audio descriptions for online videos. However, a majority of videos available online do not have audio descriptions, meaning that there is clearly still more work to be done to ensure equitable access to the internet.

Integrated Description versus Separate Audio Files versus Text-Based Description

Integrated Description

There are three main ways to add audio descriptions to a video. One method, sometimes referred to as *integrated description,* involves incorporating narrated descriptions of visual elements into the primary audio track of the video. With this method all users will experience the audio descriptions. This can be done in more than one way. For example, in some cases it might be possible to naturally incorporate all of the important visual elements into the video narration. In a tutorial demonstrating how to complete a task, if all elements of the visuals in the video are also described in the audio, this is an example of integrated description.

The other main way of offering integrated description in a video is to add video descriptions to the natural pauses in the narrative or dialogue of the main audio track. These descriptions are often recorded in a different voice from the main speech or narration to make it clear which content is description and which is the main audio. In this approach, all users will experience the audio descriptions, and they will sound more like a traditional set of audio descriptions than in the first version of integrated description. In this way, this approach can be particularly useful when working with platforms that do not support the inclusion of alternative audio tracks for video descriptions. At the same time, this approach means that users have no option to opt out of hearing the audio descriptions. While this method will improve access for those who cannot see the video content, especially because it does not require that they know how to access a separate audio track, it can also be distracting or confusing for other users.

Separate Audio Files

As a second method, audio descriptions can be offered in a separate audio file that can be selected or deselected in a manner similar to closed captions. This method improves accessibility for those who are helped by audio descriptions, but does require a video delivery platform that both supports separate audio tracks and also offers an accessible way to listen to these audio tracks. Each of these aspects is important. Not all online video platforms offer the ability to have alternative audio tracks, and at the same time, not all online video platforms are completely accessible, so it is important to consider both of these factors when determining which approach to audio descriptions is appropriate in a particular setting. In the case of platforms that do meet these two criteria, this approach to audio descriptions offers greater flexibility and customizability so users can access the information in the way that best fits their needs.

Text-Based Description

Alternatively, with some media players, it is possible to provide descriptions as text files that are read aloud using either built-in browser functionality or a screen reader. This third method does not require the describer to create a recording of the descriptions, but it does require that the file have time stamps to synchronize the reading of the descriptions with the video. Often these descriptions are made available as WebVTT files. In some cases, users can set their preferences so the video will automatically pause when the descriptions are read.

Best Practices in the Creation of Audio Description

By their very nature, audio descriptions are quite subjective. Unlike captions, which try to recreate the soundtrack, the heart of audio description is determining which visual elements are important and the optimal way to describe them. Because the goal generally is for the audio descriptions to fit within the natural pauses in the audio track, a major task for anyone creating audio descriptions is to decide what information is important and convey it in a concise manner. This makes audio description a creative process. As Joel Snyder states:

> Audio Description is a kind of literary art form in itself, to a great extent. . . . It provides a verbal version of the visual—the visual is made verbal, and aural, and oral. Using words that are succinct, vivid, and imaginative, AD conveys the visual image that is not fully accessible to a segment of the population and not fully realized by the rest of us—the rest of us, sighted folks who see but who may not observe.[17]

Because of this element of creativity, it can be difficult to boil the creation of audio description down to a series of rote steps. Instead it is a process that requires practice and refinement over time. For this reason, many audio descriptions are created by professional audio describers.

However, there are best practices that can help to ensure that the audio descriptions will be effective in providing access:

- It is helpful to always explicitly consider what is missing from the experience of the video if sound is the only point of access. It can be easy to slip away from this point of view, so audio describers, particularly those who are new to the process, should start their description process by carefully considering this aspect. Some questions to consider:

    - Who is visible?
    - Who is speaking?
    - What is happening silently on the screen or is happening with sounds that do not make the action obvious?
    - Are silent elements conveying information? These can include facial expressions, gestures, and text shown on the screen but not spoken.

- Because time is always a factor in descriptions, particularly descriptions that must fit within the natural pauses in the original audio track, prioritization is key. It is vital to understand what the most important information is and focus on clearly conveying that information.
- Be as concise as possible. The goal is not to fill each and every pause, but instead to convey the necessary information as briefly and clearly as possible. As Sabine Braun notes,

    > It can be assumed that sighted viewers do not process everything they see. . . . In other words, the visual mode is rather impressionistic. By contrast, the sequential nature of the verbal mode seems to encourage a more complete processing of the information offered. Extensive descriptions can, therefore, lead to a cognitive processing overload in the recipient.[18]

- Context is important. The setting may be important, for example, in a film, but may be less important in other works, such as educational videos that perhaps have no other setting than a close-up of a chalkboard or a set of slides. Thus, while the setting should likely always be offered, the amount of detail provided will vary.
- Text shown on screen should always be included in audio descriptions, as it will not be accessible otherwise.
- Do not offer commentary or flourishes. Though interpretation is inherent in the description process, audio descriptions should be as objective and neutral as possible. Audio descriptions should be unobtrusive, almost fading into the background. This is particularly important in the case of dramatic works.
- Think about the audience when deciding the level of complexity for vocabulary and syntax. The audio descriptions should be aimed at the same audience as the video itself.
- As with captions, do not censor content that is not otherwise censored or obscured in the video. The goal is to offer those using audio descriptions the same access to the content as other audience members.
- Audio describing requires practice, both in the sense that describers will likely have to write, refine, and even practice the script for each project and also in the sense that it takes practice across multiple projects to gain this skill.

Though the creation of audio description can be less straightforward than the creation of captions, it is equally important. Without descriptions, videos with visual elements that are vital to complete comprehension and appreciation will exclude some users. As a result, it is important that audio descriptions be included in the process of developing accessible videos.

Notes

1. US Access Board, "Information and Communication Technology (ICT) Standards and Guidelines, Notice of Proposed Rulemaking, 36 CFR Parts 1193 and 1194," February 2015, 157, https://www.access-board.gov/attachments/article/1702/ict-proposed-rule.pdf (page discontinued).
2. Web Accessibility Initiative, "Understanding Success Criterion 1.2.5: Audio Description (Prerecorded)," Web Content Accessibility Guidelines 2.1, W3C, accessed October 24, 2020, https://www.w3.org/WAI/WCAG21/Understanding/audio-description-prerecorded.html.
3. National Federation for the Blind, "Blindness Statistics," January 2019, https://www.nfb.org/resources/blindness-statistics.
4. Joel Snyder, "Audio Description: The Visual Made Verbal," *International Congress Series* 1282 (September 2005): 937.
5. Federal Communications Commission, "Audio Description," May 21, 2020, https://www.fcc.gov/audio-description.
6. Department of Justice, Civil Rights Division, "Nondiscrimination on the Basis of Disability by Public Accommodations: Movie Theaters; Movie Captioning and Audio Description," Final Rule, 28 CFR Part 36, CRT Docket No. 126, AG Order No. RIN 1190-AA63, November 21, 2016, https://www.ada.gov/regs2016/movie_rule.htm.
7. Elisa Edelberg, "Legal Requirements for Audio Description," 3Play Media, last updated June 3, 2019, https://www.3playmedia.com/2017/03/22/legal-requirements-audio-description.
8. Web Accessibility Initiative, "Understanding Success Criterion 1.2.3: Audio Description or Media

Alternative (Prerecorded)," Web Content Accessibility Guidelines 2.1, W3C, accessed October 24, 2020, https://www.w3.org/WAI/WCAG21/Understanding/audio-description-or-media-alternative-prerecorded.
9. Web Accessibility Initiative, "Understanding Success Criterion 1.2.5."
10. Web Accessibility Initiative, "Understanding Success Criterion 1.2.8: Media Alternative (Prerecorded)," Web Content Accessibility Guidelines 2.1, W3C, accessed October 24, 2020, https://www.w3.org/WAI/WCAG21/Understanding/media-alternative-prerecorded.html.
11. "Blind and Deaf at Movie: One Hundred Applaud Talking Film at Special Showing," *New York Times*, August 28, 1929, 28.
12. Jaclyn Packer, Katie Vizenor, and Joshua A. Miele, "An Overview of Video Description: History, Benefits, and Guidelines," *Journal of Visual Impairment and Blindness* 109, no. 2 (2015): 84.
13. Snyder, "Audio Description," 936.
14. Packer, Vizenor, and Miele, "Overview of Video Description," 85.
15. Packer, Vizenor, and Miele, "Overview of Video Description," 85.
16. Packer, Vizenor, and Miele. "Overview of Video Description," 85.
17. Snyder, "Audio Description," 936–37.
18. Sabine Braun, "Audiodescription Research: State of the Art and Beyond," *Translation Studies in the New Millennium* 6 (2008): 21.

Chapter 5

Other Considerations for Video Accessibility

Though closed captioning, transcripts, and audio descriptions are important to the creation of accessible video content, they are not the only accessibility features that are relevant to this medium. This chapter discusses some other important considerations for ensuring that videos are accessible for all users.

Sign Language Interpretation

Another option for improving accessibility in a video is providing sign language interpretation. There can be several reasons why this approach is preferable to captions or transcripts in at least some situations. First, in the case of American Sign Language (ASL), it can provide greater access than English captions or transcripts. ASL is its own separate natural language with a syntax and grammar different from English. This means that a D/deaf viewer may be fluent in ASL, but may not be as comfortable reading English captions, particularly at the speed required to follow a video. Second, including professional ASL interpretation can seamlessly convey tone and inflection in a way that is more difficult and awkward in captions. Finally, in some cases, particularly live streaming events, a professional ASL interpreter could provide more accessible real-time interpretation of the event than would live captioning, particularly if an automatic transcription or captioning tool was being used instead of a stenocaptioner.

When considering professional sign language interpretation, there are a few best practices to keep in mind:

- Even if auto-captions are available for an online event, it is helpful to offer a process for requesting sign language interpretation in advance. If this option is offered, it is important to have clear instructions on how to place such a request and a deadline that leaves enough time to schedule a professional interpreter.
- Following along from that first point, it is important to schedule an interpreter far in advance of the event so that it is possible to find a qualified interpreter; leaving this to the last minute prior to the event may result in inadequate services.
- If the event is presented live to an audience (for example, in an auditorium) in addition to being streamed for online viewing, ensure that the interpreter is clearly visible in the recording. When possible, it can be worth devoting a separate camera to the interpreter when the interpretation will be included in a recording.
- When the event will be purely online, the placement of the interpreter is still vital. Typically, online event systems such as videoconferencing tools will offer the option to have a separate video for the interpreter. It is important to ensure that the captions and comments boxes, if any, do not obscure the view of the interpreter.
- Keep in mind that most events will be long enough to require team interpretation, which means that multiple interpreters will work in shifts of a set time.
- When designing recorded video content, consider whether there are options for creating videos with sign language instead of or in addition to captions. For example, some institutions offer recordings of sign language tours to expand access.

While sign language interpretation is often seen as unnecessary when captions are provided, in reality it offers another access point that can improve accessibility for many viewers and also offers them a more welcoming experience. It is worth considering, particularly for live events, even if there are plans in place to offer captions.

Flashing Elements in Video and Photosensitive Epilepsy

Another aspect of accessibility that impacts videos as well as animations is the restriction against flashing elements, which may trigger photosensitive epileptic seizures or other physical reactions in users. These reactions can be caused both by flashing light and by patterns that consist of high contrast light and dark elements. With respect to patterned elements, the reaction is typically caused when the patterns are flashing or moving rapidly. Though this is not a common issue, it does happen even in commercial media. For example, in 2018, Pixar re-edited *The Incredibles 2* after receiving reports that some scenes featuring strobe and flashing lights might cause issues for viewers with photosensitive epilepsy.

For the approximately one in every 4,000 people in the population who have photosensitive epilepsy, flashing elements can cause seizures.[1] Even for viewers who do not have photosensitive epilepsy, these elements can sometimes cause negative reactions, from disorientation or general discomfort to nausea and vertigo, making for an unpleasant viewing experience. This makes it imperative that videos be screened for this content and a warning be offered to viewers, ideally in multiple places, such as the text surrounding the video online, the metadata for the video, and on screen in the video. It is important to make sure that any in-video warning appears before the first instance of the flashing element.

The factors that are important in determining whether video elements will be an issue are the rate of the flashes, the amount of the screen that features the content in question, and, particularly in the case of patterns, the contrast between the elements. WCAG 2.1 has two Success Criteria related to this issue that explain what is required for safe online content:

- Success Criterion 2.3.1, which is required for Level A compliance, states, "Web pages do not contain anything that flashes more than three times in any one second period, or the flash is below the general flash and red flash thresholds."
- Success Criterion 2.3.2, which is required for Level AAA compliance, states, "Web pages do not contain anything that flashes more than three times in any one second period."[2]

The process of evaluating videos for problematic content can be at least partially automated, and a tool for that process is discussed in the next chapter.

Media Player Accessibility

Even if the video itself is made accessible, the content can still be completely inaccessible to users if the media player used to display the content is inaccessible. This fact makes it important to focus on selecting a video player that works well for all users. Not all of the tools commonly available offer full accessibility, so it is important not to assume that a tool will be accessible without careful consideration. While it is, of course, possible to code an accessible media player, there are also a number of different accessible media players that are open source or free, so advanced programming skills are not necessary to offer an accessible video experience. The next chapter will include details on some of these accessible media players.

For those evaluating media players, there are some accessibility features to pay particular attention to:

- Whether the video autoplays without user input. Videos should not play automatically because this can be an accessibility issue, particularly for users who may not know where the audio is coming from, such as blind users. At a minimum, the media player should offer an option to disable autoplay.
- The option to turn captions on and off and, ideally, customize the display of the captions.
- The option to turn audio descriptions on and off.
- Transcripts should be available in an accessible manner, regardless of whether they are interactive or not.
- Transcripts should be searchable and, ideally, crawlable by search engine. Crawlability is not necessary for access to the video content itself, but it will simplify the process of searching for relevant videos that are accessible.
- All controls for the media player should be able to be used through keyboard commands and voice input so that they are usable by those who do not use a mouse. Ideally, they should be optimized to support this use, including features such as a visual and/or audio indication of which element has keyboard focus at any given time.
- All controls for the media player should be large enough that they can be comfortably clicked on by mouse users without requiring high levels of manual dexterity.
- There should be no "keyboard traps," meaning that users who navigate via keyboard should always be able to navigate away from any elements, including controls and interactive content.
- The elements of the media player should be labeled appropriately and of visually high contrast.
- The speed of the video should be customizable for those who require or prefer slower or faster speeds to support comprehension.

Evaluation of media players is important regardless of whether the evaluation pertains to an application used to embed videos into websites, a platform for hosting videos, or a database or other proprietary platform that includes videos.

Designing Accessible Video Content

When creating video content, it is important to also keep in mind how design choices within the video content can impact accessibility. Many of these features are similar to those that make all kinds of designs accessible, but it can be easy to overlook them when creating video content. It is important to integrate accessibility considerations into the process of creating video to ensure that it will be accessible to all. One should remember the following:

- Lighting is important. Scenes that are too dimly lit can be inaccessible to those with low vision and generally difficult for all users, depending on the lighting where the video is watched (for example, glare when watching content outdoors).
- Contrast matters in video just as it does in print media and online. This issue can be related to lighting, but it is worth pointing out that contrast is also important when the video includes text on a background, such as when a slide presentation is displayed.
- Elements should be large enough to be clear. Small text or tiny details may not be viewable to those with low vision or when the video is displayed at certain sizes (for example, on mobile devices).
- Color should not be used as the sole way to convey information in the video as it can exclude those who are color-blind.
- Certain motion techniques and effects should be used cautiously. Parallax scrolling, 3-D effects, and other motion effects can cause discomfort for some users who have vestibular sensitivity. These users may experience dizziness, motion sickness, or nausea in extreme situations. For this reason, it is worth considering testing with users when employing these types of effects.
- Fonts should be selected for accessibility and easy readability, which generally means avoiding decorative fonts that are more difficult to read due to their design features.

Keeping these factors in mind when creating video content will help make sure it is effective and engaging for all users. These accessibility features will help to meet the needs of a wide range of potential users, which will expand the audience of users for the videos and ensure that all viewers are able to access the videos and the information being conveyed within them.

Notes

1. G. F. A. Harding and P. F. Harding, “Photosensitive Epilepsy and Image Safety,” *Applied Ergonomics* 41, no. 4 (2010): 504–8.
2. Andrew Kirkpatrick, Joshue O Connor, Alastair Campbell, and Michal Cooper, eds., “Web Content Accessibility Guidelines (WCAG) 2.1,” W3C, June 5, 2018, https://www.w3.org/TR/WCAG21.

Chapter 6

Video Accessibility Tools

Given the popularity of online video, it makes sense that there are a wide variety of tools and organizations that focus on making video content accessible. This chapter is not intended as a comprehensive list of all available tools in this space, nor are the tools featured necessarily the best tools for each situation. Rather, this chapter is intended to provide examples of some of the popular tools used to make videos accessible and the most common workflows that institutions have developed to improve video accessibility. The list also offers an overview of the types of functions and features that are generally supported by existing tools.

In-House Video Creation

For institutions interested in creating captions, transcripts, or audio descriptions in-house, there are several tools that can support this process. They offer various advantages and disadvantages, but all will allow for the creation of accessibility features by individuals with varying degrees of technical skills at the institution itself.

CADET (Caption and Description Editing Tool)—The National Center for Accessible Media at WGBH has been a leader in media accessibility since its founding in the early 1990s. CADET is its latest tool for captioning and audio describing online media. It is a free, browser-based tool, can be used offline, and allows users to generate both caption files in multiple formats and scripts for audio descriptions. CADET was designed in a manner that protects privacy, since it "runs locally in any Web browser, so users do not need to upload private videos or proprietary content to servers or video-hosting sites in order to create captions."[1] It supports multiple types of use, including transcribing audio within the platform, importing files for editing, adding time stamps, and creating an audio description script with the proper time stamps built into it. The end product can be exported in a range of file types, including WebVTT, SRT, and plain text. In addition, CADET offers extensive documentation, tutorials, and a user group, which make it relatively easy to learn to use the platform and to offer feedback that can impact its future.

YouDescribe—This free tool, developed by the Smith-Kettlewell Eye Research Institute, offers a way for anyone to add audio descriptions to existing YouTube videos regardless of whether they are the owner or creator of the video. To do this, YouDescribe offers recording functionality so that registered users can record audio descriptions for the video that are timed to the appropriate points in the video. The description is then offered on the YouDescribe platform, which is synchronized with the underlying YouTube video. Viewers have the option to modify the balance between the volume of the video's original soundtrack and the audio description soundtrack. From the viewer's perspective, YouDescribe offers options to search through described content, post videos to the Wish List to request that they be described, and even rate a user's descriptions. All videos can be shared via the integrated sharing feature or URL. YouDescribe offers both written and video tutorials and the ability to contact the site for support. The tool is entirely browser-based and works with most modern browsers. YouDescribe has also debuted an iOS app for watching, requesting, and providing feedback on videos.

YouTube—YouTube is a well-known video hosting platform, and it has also been known for its captioning features for some time. The platform offers multiple ways to caption videos. It offers a free automatic captioning function, which will generate captions using its AI captioning feature once a video is uploaded to the platform. Unfortunately, as with virtually all automatic captioning features, these captions often have significant errors and are rarely, if ever, of a quality that is sufficient to provide equitable access to the video content without additional editing. However, the automated captions usually provide a good starting point, which can then be edited, making the process more efficient than creating captions from scratch. YouTube also includes other tools to make captioning easier. A video creator can upload a previously prepared script, which is then automatically synchronized with the video. Video creators who wish to create captions from scratch can transcribe the video directly in the YouTube platform. Creators have fine control over the captions and can set the number of words that appear on the screen at any time, when they appear, and how long they stay on the screen. The transcription tool also pauses video automatically as captions are being typed, making the process easier. YouTube also allows users to download finished captions in several file formats, which means that it can be used to automatically generate and edit captions, even if YouTube is not the final destination for the video file.

Amara—As a project that is affiliated with the Participatory Culture Foundation and a nonprofit, Amara is another option for captioning projects. Unlike CADET, Amara is specifically focused on captions and subtitles. In fact, one of its primary functions is to facilitate translating and subtitling video content. These same features can be used for creating captions. One of the advantages of Amara is that it is specifically designed to facilitate collaboration by a team on a single video, which can be helpful for workflows that involve multiple individuals. Through its Amara On Demand segment, the organization also offers professional captioning and translation and subtitling. The platform also offers the option to volunteer to caption or subtitle videos as part of a number of teams that remediate videos either for specific organizations, such as the Ellen MacArthur Foundation, *Ability* magazine, Mozilla, *Scientific American*, and DoiT International, to name just a few, or at the request of D/deaf or hard-of-hearing individuals. Amara offers the ability to export captions in a variety of file formats and has a support site that covers each of the pieces of the platform.

While this selection of tools has features that can facilitate many of the functions that libraries may want to undertake, there are many reasons that institutions may consider other options, whether these are other current tools or newly emerging technologies. When selecting a tool for creating captions, transcripts, and audio descriptions, some key factors are

- the cost of the platform and whether this price can change frequently;
- the quality of any documentation and any customer support services that are offered;
- the ease with which multiple parties can collaborate on files;
- the variety of different file types and which file types are available for exporting the end product; and
- the flexibility of the tool to work on multiple devices and with multiple browsers.

Vendors for Outsourcing Video Accessibility Features

For some institutions, or at least for some types of content, it can be preferable to outsource the creation of captions, transcripts, audio descriptions, or some combination of these features. In the case of some subscription services, the option to request that video content in the subscription be captioned, transcribed, or described may be a part of the platform. However, there are also vendors that accept submissions of video content for captioning, transcriptions, and description on any platform.

3Play Media—Offering captioning, transcription, subtitling, and audio description, 3Play Media can cover a whole range of video needs. It guarantees 99 percent accuracy and fast turnaround times, though some expedited turnaround options may cost more than its standard service. In addition to these services, it offers the 3Play Plugin, which it says allows users to integrate accessibility content into media players that do not have native support for the content, and includes APIs that can help integrate submitting content to 3Play Media into existing workflows. It can also support over twenty different languages, which is helpful for organizations that produce or maintain multilingual content. End users have the ability to edit captions and audio descriptions created by the company, and it can support both open and closed captions. For those hosting live events, it also offers live auto-captioning features that integrate with Zoom, YouTube, Facebook, and more. In addition to its services, its website also features a wealth of information about video accessibility, including white papers, webinars, how-to guides, and a blog, and it also offers an online video accessibility course.

Rev—Another company that offers captions and transcripts, Rev promises 99 percent accuracy with its transcription and captioning services but also offers a less expensive "Rough Draft" option that guarantees 80 percent accuracy and is machine-generated transcription. Rev can offer automatic live captions for Zoom meetings and foreign language subtitles in more than eight languages as well. It features integration with Dropbox and Google Drive to streamline workflows and offers both quicker turnaround times and verbatim transcription at a higher cost. It also offers webinars, tutorials, how-to guides, and more on its website.

Verbit—For those interested in taking advantage of the ever-improving capabilities of artificial intelligence, Verbit uses its own proprietary, AI-powered automatic captioning technology to create transcripts, which are then reviewed by its team. It guarantees 99 percent accuracy of the end result. Verbit has current integrations with both learning management systems—such as Blackboard, Canvas, and Brightcove—and video hosting platforms, such as Panopto, YouTube, Vimeo, and VoiceThread. It also offers real-time auto-captioning using the same technology it uses for transcription. Its website includes additional support resources, including a blog, webinars, and guides.

Otter.ai—This auto-transcription tool can be used to generate transcripts that can then also be used to create video captions. It can support both automatic transcription of files that are uploaded to the platform and live auto-transcription within Zoom and other live events. The pricing model has options for individuals, educational institutions, and businesses, and there is a free tier for individuals. It also offers discounted pricing for students and teachers using their educational e-mail accounts. Because the transcription is completely automated, the accuracy may not be as high as some of the other tools discussed.

In addition to these companies and other large-scale vendors in this area, other smaller vendors may specialize in specific types of content, individual accessibility features (such as audio descriptions), or specific geographic regions. When selecting a vendor, some institutions may decide to go through a full RFP process. Generally, when evaluating vendors, one should ask the following key questions:

- What is the cost of their services, and how is the pricing determined (for example, by minute of the video)?
- What is the turnaround time for their services?
- What level of accuracy is guaranteed, and what are the available remedies if a video does not meet their standards?
- How do they address technical terminology, foreign language content, and other content that can require specialized expertise?
- What is the process for submitting content to them?
- What file formats do they offer and support?
- Are they integrated into any platforms?
- Do they offer an API?

Identifying Seizure-Triggering Content

Photosensitive Epilepsy Analysis Tool (PEAT)—Created by the Trace Center at the University of Maryland, PEAT is a free tool that helps to identify content that is high risk for causing photosensitive seizures. It works for both videos and animations, but does require access to a PC running Windows 10, Windows 7, Windows Vista, or Windows XP.

Accessible Media Players

When sharing video online, making the video accessible through captions, transcripts, and audio descriptions is only part of the process. Without the use of an accessible media player, this content may still be inaccessible to many users. It is possible to develop a custom media player that meets accessibility standards, but there are also existing options that can streamline the process of sharing video in a way that works for a wide range of users.

OzPlayer—This media player puts accessibility at the forefront of its work. It asserts that it was the first fully accessible media player and that it is compliant with WCAG 2.0, Level AA.[2] It also continues to update its code frequently to ensure continued functionality and accessibility. OzPlayer is an HTML5-based media player that supports captions, transcripts, audio descriptions, and keyboard access. The tool is a commercial product, but it is "free for personal use and for not-for-profits with annual budgets under $1,000,000 (USD)."[3]

Able Player—Another accessible media player is the HTML5-based Able Player, which is free and open source. It supports a wide range of accessibility features, including captions, interactive transcripts, multiple approaches to audio description, keyboard navigation, and adjustable playback rates. Able Player supports more than a dozen languages and offers multiple ways for users with various expertise to contribute to the project.

One should remember, however, that even if a media player is accessible, the site where it is hosted should be tested for accessibility and compliance with WCAG 2.1.

Notes

1. National Center for Accessible Media, "CADET—Caption and Descriptive Editing Tool," WGBH, https://www.wgbh.org/foundation/what-we-do/ncam/cadet.
2. OzPlayer, AccessibilityOz, https://www.accessibilityoz.com/ozplayer.
3. OzPlayer.

Chapter 7

Video Accessibility Workflows

Video accessibility can involve several different workflows depending on whether video is being evaluated or created. To ensure that video content is accessible, it is necessary to evaluate both content that the library purchases or subscribes to from outside vendors and content created, preserved, or maintained by the library directly. There are several workflows that can help to ensure accessibility is not overlooked and provide the structure needed for remediating videos that are not currently accessible. These workflows are intended as starting points for this process, though they may need to be refined or modified depending on specific institutional needs.

Evaluating Video Purchases and Subscriptions

When developing workflows around accessibility evaluation for collection development purposes, it is important to include an evaluation of video content in the library's collection. The first step in this process is to request a Voluntary Product Accessibility Template (VPAT) from the vendor, if one has not already been provided. A VPAT is a document that explains how an item, such as a database or piece of software, does or does not satisfy the requirements of a particular accessibility standard. Typical standards that are included are

- Web Content Accessibility Guidelines (WCAG), which is the international standard for web content accessibility;
- Revised Section 508 standards, which govern software and hardware procured by the US federal government and is often used as a standard by other institutions as well; and
- EN 301 549 accessibility requirements, which govern public procurement of ICT products and services across the EU.

VPATs are generally organized by WCAG success criteria, which makes it relatively straightforward to have a process in place for specifically checking video accessibility. The relevant success criteria to focus on for video content are those found in 1.2 Time-Based Media, which covers the requirements for video accessibility to meet Level A, Level AA, and Level AAA conformance levels.[1]

Unfortunately, VPATs are not always accurate. A 2015 study of VPATs found an "inaccuracy rate of 19.6%."[2] This means that it is worthwhile to make an independent verification of accessibility features part of the evaluation process. While often accessibility evaluations make use of automated testing tools, in the case of video, it isn't possible to fully assess all accessibility features in this way. While these tools can be used for certain elements of the process, as discussed further below, at least at this point, they cannot evaluate the adequacy of captions and audio descriptions. This means that manual verification is necessary to ensure accessibility of video content.

Evaluating Captions

Because captions are integrated into video files, the best way to evaluate captions is by watching the video. For purposes of evaluating a vendor resource, this may mean checking a few videos to confirm that captions are consistently high quality. The following questions can guide this review:

- Are captions present in all videos with sound elements that are integral to understanding the video?
- Are the captions synchronized with the video and its soundtrack?
- Do the captions achieve 99 percent accuracy? If not, estimate how accurate they are to determine adequacy.
- Do the captions indicate who is speaking and whether the speaker is on screen or off screen?

- Are non-dialogue sounds captioned appropriately?
- Can the captions be turned on and off (e.g., closed versus open captions)?
- Are the captions high contrast enough to read over the video?
- Is the font clear, customizable, or both?
- Can the font color of the captions be changed?
- Can the font size of the captions be changed?
- Can the background of the captions be changed?
- Can the captions be moved to another location on the video? If not, does the layout ensure that they do not obscure the video?
- Do the captions censor or otherwise skip important content?
- Overall, are the captions sufficient to allow the user to completely understand the video without the soundtrack?
- Are captions immediately available on new content as it is added to the platform? If not, how quickly is it added, and is there an option to place a request to expedite this process if needed?
- Are the controls for the video (i.e., play, pause, audio levels, toggle for captions) accessible?

Evaluating Transcripts

Because transcripts are not integrated into the video file itself, the process for evaluating their accessibility is a bit different. This will require both an evaluation of the transcript text and an evaluation of the area displaying the transcripts to ensure that both are accessible. Evaluating the area displaying the transcript can largely be tested via automated accessibility testing tools, at least to the same extent as other web content. Transcript text, unfortunately, is less amenable to automated testing tools and needs to be evaluated manually at this point. It also requires checking a few video transcripts to confirm they are consistently high quality. The following questions can help in the evaluation process:

- Does the transcript accurately capture the sound elements in the video?
- Does the transcript include necessary descriptions of key visual elements, represented clearly in a manner so that they are not mistaken for part of the audio track?
- Are there elements that require transcripts, such as sound elements, visual elements, or a combination of the two, that are integral to understanding the video?
- For scrolling or highlighted transcripts, is the motion in synchronization with the video and its soundtrack?
- For interactive transcripts, does searching in or clicking on sections of the transcript move the user to the appropriate point in the video?
- Is the transcript in a usable font size and style? Is the font customizable?
- Is the transcript searchable? This feature makes the transcripts more usable for a wider range of users.
- Is the transcript exportable? While this is not absolutely necessary for accessibility, it does make it easier to use the transcript in more ways and for more purposes.
- Is the interface in which the transcript is presented accessible to assistive devices and by keyboard navigation?

Evaluating Audio Descriptions

As with captions and transcripts, it is often necessary to play a video file, or a sample of videos, to evaluate whether audio descriptions are present and whether they are adequate. In some cases, when audio descriptions are listed as a separate audio track or a separate version of the video, it may be clear that the platform offers audio descriptions, but it is still important to manually examine their adequacy. The following questions can guide the evaluation process:

- Are the audio descriptions part of the main audio track or a separate audio track? If the latter, are users able to turn them on or off?
- Are the audio descriptions audible? For audio descriptions that are part of a separate audio track, can the volume for the audio descriptions be adjusted separately from the main audio track?
- Are the audio descriptions at a speed that is comprehensible?
- Do the audio descriptions fit within the natural pauses without overlapping any key elements of the soundtrack?
- Do the audio descriptions adequately convey visual elements in a way that makes the video understandable by those not watching the video?

While it may not be possible to evaluate every single video file included in a platform, this evaluation process can be done with a small sample of videos. If videos are presented in multiple formats, it would be worthwhile to check the different formats as part of this process. As this evaluation is being done, an important piece of the workflow is also documentation. Keeping notes about the results of the review will help in a few ways. First, it makes it possible to offer guidance to users on what is and is not available. Second, it can help when following up to determine whether accessibility has improved or deteriorated. Finally, this evaluation can be made a part of the collection development decision-making process more easily if there is documentation. It can also be useful when negotiating with a vendor and, when appropriate, the results shared with the vendor as a way of advocating for improved features.

Creating Accessible Video Content

There are many different approaches that libraries can take to incorporating accessibility in videos created in-house, from creating accessibility features internally to outsourcing the work to any one of many different services that caption or describe audio content for a fee. Depending on the nature of the video to be captioned, the time line for creating captions, and the available staff time and skills, different approaches may make more or less sense for a particular institution or project, but these workflows offer options that can be customized for individual institutional needs.

Creating Captions and Transcripts from a Script

One of the easiest ways of creating captions and transcripts is from an existing script. Having an accurate script on hand can streamline the process considerably, but there are still several steps to the workflow:

- Create a script before the video is created, and then record the video.
- Once the video is recorded, correct the script to reflect any deviations from the script during recording.
- Save the script in an appropriate file format. While the exact file formats that will work depend on the platform you are using, SubRip (.srt) and WebVTT (.vtt) are common options that are available across many platforms.
- Upload this file with the video in a platform that supports closed captions, or use video editing software to incorporate open captions into the video.
- In the case of captions or interactive transcripts, check that the file has synchronized properly so that the correct text is displayed at the correct time stamp in the video.

While this process is one of the most efficient ways of adding captions or transcripts to a video, it depends heavily on whether a script has been created and is closely followed in the process of creating the video. This will not be practical in all cases, and, if the script will not be accurate when uploaded, this approach may not necessarily save time in the process.

Editing Automatically Generated Captions and Transcripts

While automatic captions and transcripts are not yet able to reach the accuracy levels needed to provide full access to video content, they can be used as a starting point for creating more accurate captions when a script is not available. This workflow can be used for that process.

- Once the video file is completed, upload it to a service that automatically captions videos. There are many options, including YouTube, Facebook, and Otter.ai. It is important to note that once the video has been uploaded, it can take some time for the automatic captions to be generated. This is generally not an instantaneous process, and the timing can be variable, particularly with free tools, in some cases taking up to several days before captions are generated.
- Assign an individual to review the automatically generated captions. Though this may not seem like a difficult task, it can be time-consuming, especially for those who are new to the process. It tends to be a bit faster when done by the person who created the video or the main speaker in the video, as this streamlines understanding the content in the video. It is also a process where experience can increase speed.
- Review and correct the captions with a focus on the following:
    - *Punctuation*—Often automatic captioning and transcription tools miss important punctuation, and some, such as YouTube, tend not to insert punctuation at all.
    - *Grammar*—Sometimes the speech recognition tools used for this purpose will introduce grammar errors, so it is important to make corrections to ensure that the grammar matches the audio track.
    - *Spelling*—This can be one of the most important aspects of the correction process. Spelling errors will happen most frequently with words that sound very similar to other words, where a proper name is not in the tool's dictionary, when foreign words are used, and where the speech being captioned is accented.
- Add any non-speech sounds that are not included automatically. Generally these are added in square brackets, but some organizations use parentheses. Though square brackets are the best practice, the most important consideration is that these are used consistently within a video and, ideally, across videos at an institution.

- Insert line breaks to ensure that the captions are readable. Generally, a caption should have no more than eight to ten words on a line, though the exact number will depend on word length. Also, it is best to limit the number of lines on the screen at one time so that the captions do not block the video.
- Check and correct timing as necessary. Though automatic captioning tools try to keep the captions synchronous with the video, there may be errors, and it is important to make sure that the captions are synchronized and remain on the screen for the appropriate length of time.
- Once these corrections have been made, save and, if required by the tool being used, publish the corrected captions.
- An optional step in this process is to have another member of the team double-check videos for accuracy. This can be helpful for ensuring accuracy, particularly for those who are new to captioning or transcribing. This process could be applied to all videos, or a few videos could be spot-checked at random.
- A final optional step in this process is to download and archive the finished file so that it can be backed up separately from the platform used to create it (or available for archiving or uploading to other platforms as necessary).

While editing automatically generated captions and transcripts is a significant undertaking, it really cannot be overlooked. Without corrections, these automatically generated texts do not provide the level of accuracy necessary for accessibility. For this reason, it is very important to factor in the staff time required for this process when determining the budget for captions and when deciding which approach to video accessibility the institution will create.

Creating Audio Descriptions

As discussed in chapter 4, the process of creating audio descriptions requires skill and experience. Because they should ideally fit into the natural pauses in the existing audio track and because they require judgments about what content needs to be described, creating audio descriptions is more difficult in some ways than creating captions or a transcript that simply reproduces the exact language spoken in a video. For this reason, it should be expected that the process will take a significant amount of time and will likely include all of the following steps:

- Watch the video in its entirety. Even if the person creating the audio descriptions also created the video, it is worthwhile to watch the entire video with an eye toward which visual elements should be described and when descriptions will fit. During this first viewing, some notes may be taken, but that may need to wait until a second viewing.
- Once the person creating the audio descriptions has watched the video and taken some initial notes, that same person should be tasked with creating a script of the audio description. This process should be undertaken by the same person who initially started the planning process so they are familiar with the video in its entirety, or, at a minimum, the entire section they are responsible for describing.
- The process of creating this script will likely require viewing segments of the video again and noting the time and length of gaps in the sound track. While the creation of audio descriptions cannot be automated, there are tools that can help with identifying these gaps, such as CADET, discussed in further detail in the previous chapter. The final script should denote the time markers at which the audio descriptions should start and stop.
- Once the script is drafted, it should ideally be reviewed for clarity by a separate party to ensure that it provides meaningful access to all necessary visual content.
- The person tasked with recording the audio descriptions should review the script. The person recording the audio description need not be the same person who created the script, and, in fact, there may be some value in hiring a professional voice-over artist at this point depending on the nature and scope of the process.
- The audio descriptions should be recorded per the timing listed in the script.
- The penultimate step in this process will depend on the platform. If the platform supports a second audio track with audio descriptions, this file can be uploaded at this point. In this scenario, the main audio track would need to be edited only if there was a need to lower background noises or soundtrack elements so they do not obscure the audio descriptions. However, if a separate audio description track is not supported, as is the case in many platforms, the audio description recording will need to be edited into the pauses in the main soundtrack.
- Regardless of the approach taken in the previous step, the final step is confirming that the audio descriptions are properly synchronized with the video.

Because of the divergent skills required to create the script and then record it, this workflow is more likely to involve multiple creators than the others discussed in this chapter. Given the high level of skills involved, the creation of audio description may be an area where institutions find it more effective to outsource this workflow.

Outsourcing Caption, Transcript, and Audio Description Creation

Because of the time and skill required to create accurate captions, transcripts, and audio descriptions, many organizations opt to outsource the production of these tools rather than creating them in-house. This can save staff time and, in some cases, may even be more budget-friendly, but it is important to note that this still requires a plan and workflow to proceed successfully. While each vendor offers different specific procedures, this workflow demonstrates the basic steps with a focus on where an organization will still need to allocate staff time:

- Once a video file is created, it will be submitted to the selected vendor. There are many ways this submission process can happen, including e-mailing it to the vendor, uploading it to the vendor's website, using an integrated submission feature in another platform, or even integrating it into a project via an API.
- After the vendor receives the video, it will process the video. During this step, the institution should monitor to ensure that the time frame for returning the completed captions, transcript, or audio descriptions is met.
- Completed videos must be manually reviewed for accuracy. Some vendors guarantee specific accuracy levels, but it is still important to ensure that this accuracy rate is being met. Depending on the institutional comfort level, this process could range from randomly sampling videos for review to routinely checking each video when it is returned.
- Depending on the method of submitting the video to the vendor and receiving it back, the final step of the process may include uploading the video to the desired hosting platform or media player and ensuring that the features all work as intended and are synchronized properly.

Additional workflow steps may be required depending on the specific vendor's approach and the agreement between the parties. For example, in some cases vendors charge by minute, in which case tracking the number of minutes submitted should be included as part of the workflow for budgeting and planning purposes.

Live Event Video Accessibility

Accessibility for live streaming events, particularly those that will be recorded for later distribution as recordings, is an important workflow to consider when thinking about video accessibility. These steps will help to ensure that both the event and the recording offer maximum accessibility:

- When planning an event, always include accessibility in the plan and the budget from the very beginning. Moreover, it should always be assumed that the event will attract a diverse audience with varied needs; assuming that no one with a particular need will attend is no excuse for excluding an interested participant.
- Select a streaming platform that supports accessibility. An increasing number of platforms have automatically generated captions integrated into the platform, but these suffer from the same accuracy issues as other types of automatic captions. For this reason, it is important to make sure that the platform supports having a stenocaptioner captioning the event as it happens or displaying an ASL interpreter on the screen.
- Ensure that you understand how the platform's features work together. In some cases, captions may be covered by other features, such as chat messages from participants, or the captions themselves may interfere with clearly seeing the ASL interpreter. It is important to check for these issues in advance and, where possible, configure the features and display options to avoid issues.
- Coordinate with anyone who will be speaking or presenting at the event to ensure that they know how to optimize their presentations for accessibility.
- When advertising the event, clearly state which features will be offered, such as live captioning, descriptions, or interpretation, and offer clear instructions for how to request accommodations.
- On the day of the event, have someone available for questions or issues relating to these accessibility features.
- After the event, edit any caption or transcript file for accuracy before posting the recording. Though professional stenocaptioners strive for accuracy, often there will be typographical, spelling, or other errors that need to be addressed to improve the accuracy of the file.
- When posting the recording, post any related files, such as slides that were displayed during the presentation, in an accessible format.

These steps will greatly improve accessibility of the event and the recording and ensure that the content is available to the widest possible audience.

While these workflows may represent new areas of work, they will help to ensure that current and future videos are accessible to users with a range of disabilities. This process is not only legally required in many jurisdictions, but is also vital to making institutions, their collections, and their programs truly inclusive for disabled users.

Notes

1. World Wide Web Consortium, "Time-based Media: Understanding Guideline 1.2," in Understanding WCAG 2.0: A Guide to Understanding and Implementing WCAG 2.0, 2016, https://www.w3.org/TR/UNDERSTANDING-WCAG20/media-equiv.html.
2. Laura DeLancey, "Assessing the Accuracy of Vendor-Supplied Accessibility Documentation," *Library Hi Tech* 33, no. 1 (2015), https://doi.org/10.1108/LHT-08-2014-0077.

Notes

Notes

Library Technology REPORTS

Upcoming Issues	
May/June 57:4	**Creating Adaptable Digital Preservation Workflows** by Erin Baucom
July 57:5	**Digital Repositories with Cloud Technology** by Jarrod Bogucki
August/ September 57:6	**Metadata Applications Profiles for Library Data** by Theo Gerontakos and Ben Riesenberg